WASTE, RECYCLING AND REUSE

by Sally Morgan

Evans

WWF

Published by Evans Brothers Limited
2A Portman Mansions
Chiltern Street,
London W1U 6NR

© White-Thomson Publishing Ltd 2006

Produced for Evans Brothers Limited by

White-Thomson Publishing Ltd
210 High Street,
Lewes, East Sussex
BN7 2NH

Editorial: Catherine Clarke
Design: Tinstar Design Ltd (www.tinstar.co.uk)
Consultant: Lisa Cockerton
WWF reviewers: Patricia Kendell and Cherry Duggan
Picture research: Amy Sparks

Printed in China by WKT on chlorine-free
paper from sustainably managed forests.

**British Library Cataloguing
in Publication Data.**

Morgan, Sally
   Waste, recycling and reuse. - (Sustainable futures)
   1. Refuse and refuse disposal - Juvenile literature
   2. Waste products - Juvenile literature
   3. Recycling (Waste, etc.) - Juvenile literature
   4. Sustainable development - Juvenile literature
   I. Title
   363.7'28

   ISBN-13: 9780237527709
   ISBN-10: 0237527707

WWF and the Sustainable Futures series

There are many environmental problems facing
our planet, but there is much that we can all do
to improve the situation.

WWF works to save endangered species, protect
endangered spaces and address global threats to
nature such as climate change. That is why we are
happy to be associated with the "Sustainable
Futures" series, which offers information for you
to learn from, think about and act on. Your actions
will be crucial to the future of planet Earth.

WWF-UK Registered Charity No. 1081247. A
company limited by guarantee number 4016725.
Panda symbol © 1986 WWF. ® WWF Registered
trademark.

The views of the author expressed in this publication
do not necessarily reflect those of WWF.

The author has used all reasonable endeavours to
ensure that the content of this report, the data
compiled, and the methods of calculation and
research are consistent with normally accepted
standards and practices. However, no warranty is
given to that effect nor any liability accepted by the
authors for any loss or damage arising from the use
of this report by WWF-UK or by any other party.

For further information, please contact:

WWF-UK
Panda House, Weyside Park
Godalming, Surrey GU7 1XR
Telephone: 01483 426444
Fax: 01483 426409
http://www.wwf.org.uk

Acknowledgements

The publishers would like to thank the following for
permission to reproduce photographs:
Alamy p. 38; Corbis pp. 12 (Pitchal Frederic/Corbis
Sygma), 13 (Galen Rowell), 20 (Rafiqur
Rahman/Reuters), 23 (Tom Stewart), 26 (John
Zoiner), 28 (Keren Su), 29 (Michael S. Yamashita), 34
(Strauss/Curtis), 41 (Macduff Everton), 45 (Jose Luis
Pelaez, Inc.); Digitalvision p. 36; Ecoscene pp. 6 (Erik
Schaffer), 7 (Alan Towse), 8 (Vicki Coombs), 10 (Jon
Bower), 14 (Bruce Harber), 16 (Wayne Lawler), 27
(Chinch Gryniewicz), 31 (Wayne Lawler), 32 (Tony
Page), 33 (Melanie Peters), 37 (Luc Hosten), 42
(Peter Cairns) 43 (Bruce Harber), 44 (Kevin King);
Photolibrary pp. 15 (Workbook, Inc.), pp. 17
(Photononstop), 18 (Index Stock Imagery), 21 (Lon E.
Lauber), 22 (Mark Bolton), 25 (BSIP/OSF), 30 (The
Image Works); Practical Action ITDG p. 40; Topfoto
pp. 9 (The Image Works), 35, 39 (The Image Works);
TRAID UK p. 24; WTPix p. 4.

Cover photograph reproduced with permission of
OSF/Photolibrary/Images.Com.

Contents

The waste problem

As standards of living increase around the world, people can afford to buy consumer goods such as cars, fridges, mobile phones and televisions. The manufacture of all these goods is using up the planet's resources faster than they are being produced, which means that supplies will run out. If this is to be prevented it is vitally important that the world's resources are used in a sustainable way. The word sustainable means 'the ability to continue to support itself indefinitely'. A product can be considered sustainable if its production enables the resources from which it was made to continue to be available for future generations.

Around the world, people are producing more and more waste. Developed countries in Europe and North America produce far more waste than most other countries although India and China are catching up. The least amount of waste is produced in countries such as The Gambia and Tanzania in Africa. In the past, people were more likely to repair something rather than throw it away, so goods lasted much longer. Today, people tend to throw something away when it goes wrong, often because it is cheaper to buy something new than to have repairs done.

People buy numerous electrical goods for the home. Often these items are replaced if they get damaged because it's cheaper to buy new than to pay for repairs. The design of some items can make repair almost impossible, so they have to be replaced.

Life cycles

When looking for ways of reducing waste, it is important to consider the whole life cycle of a product. The life cycle starts with the raw materials and energy used to make a product, the energy needed to transport it, and finally the way it is treated after it is used and thrown away. For example, when we buy a plastic bottle of mineral water, we drink the water and throw away the bottle. We probably do not think about the raw materials and energy that were needed to make the plastic bottle, fill it with water, transport and distribute it. We probably don't worry about what happens to it once it is thrown away, either. To get a good idea of the amount of waste we generate, and its financial and environmental costs, it is important to consider the full life cycle of products, and not just the time when they are useful to us.

Tackling waste

There is a phrase that people use to describe the ways in which the growing problem of waste can be tackled. This phrase is 'reduce, reuse and recycle'. Reduce means to stop or avoid waste production. This can mean reducing the quantity of raw materials that are used in the manufacturing process or redesigning products so that they use less material. Reuse means to put an item to a

new use, rather than to throw it away, for example, giving old clothes to a charity shop, selling unwanted items or repairing something so it can be used for longer. Recycling is the processing of used items to obtain materials that can be used to make new products.

Recycled or not?

One symbol that is used on packaging in many countries to indicate that it can be recycled is a loop that consists of three arrows arranged in a triangle. However, recently this symbol has been used to show that the product or packaging has been made using recycled materials. So the loop can mean both recycled content and that the product is recyclable. When a product is described as 'recycled', it means that it contains material that has been reprocessed. However, this does not mean that it is made from 100 per cent recycled material, so it could contain any proportion of recycled material.

This pie chart shows the make up of the rubbish in a typical UK household. Much of this rubbish can be recycled or reused. In 2000 the people of the world produced 12.6 billion tons of waste, which is 2 tons for every person. By 2050 this is expected to rise to 26.7 billion tons, which will be 3 tons per person! We all need to think of better ways of dealing with our waste before this happens.

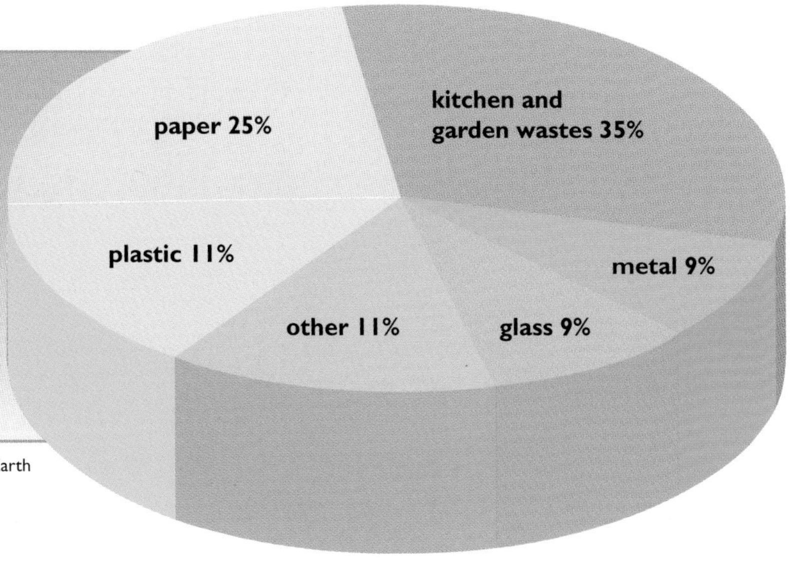

paper 25%

kitchen and garden wastes 35%

plastic 11%

metal 9%

other 11%

glass 9%

Source: Friends of the Earth

Dealing with waste

People have always produced waste, but now there are more people making more waste than ever before. There are many forms of waste including waste food, packaging, old electrical goods, broken household items, waste paper and much more. Industries, too, create large quantities of waste during the manufacture of goods. Waste is even produced when raw materials such as coal and limestone are dug from the ground.

People and waste

Historically most household waste has been dumped, buried or burned. This method of waste disposal is still common in poorer countries, especially where there are large slums or camps with no organised waste collections or sanitation. The only way these people can get rid of their waste is to dump or burn it. In developed countries, waste is collected from houses and taken to landfills or incinerators. Part of the problem in the developed world is the ease with which waste is taken away. People do not usually see where their rubbish goes, or what happens to it. So in order to reduce the amount of waste, people have to be made to think about the volume of waste that they generate.

In many countries, piles of burning rubbish are a common sight. However, rotting food can attract vermin and spread disease.

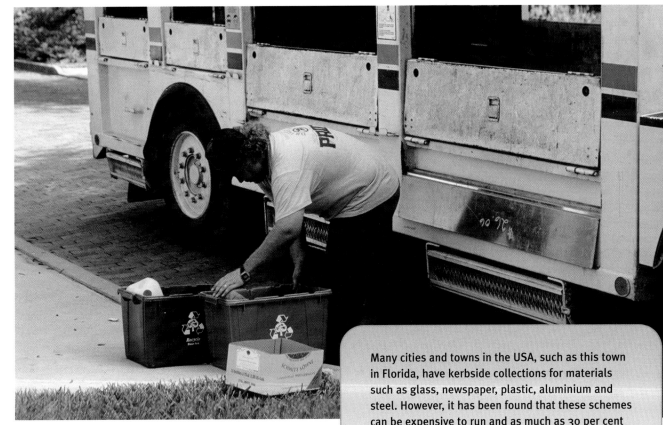

Many cities and towns in the USA, such as this town in Florida, have kerbside collections for materials such as glass, newspaper, plastic, aluminium and steel. However, it has been found that these schemes can be expensive to run and as much as 30 per cent of the materials cannot be recycled, mostly because residents dump rubbish in the recycling containers.

Pay As You Throw (PAYT)

Rubbish collections are paid for through local taxes. In most places everybody pays the same, regardless of the amount of waste they produce. This is beginning to change. In around 6000 communities across the USA there are Pay As You Throw (PAYT) schemes that charge householders for their waste collection according to the amount of waste they put out for collection. Some schemes charge for each bag or container of waste. Others charge according to the weight of the waste. These schemes are designed to encourage people to produce less waste and to recycle more. In theory, it is a fair system because people pay for the rubbish that they produce. At first, there were concerns that people would dump rubbish to avoid paying for its collection. However, in most of the places running the PAYT schemes this has not been a problem.

Getting people to recycle

If people recycle as much of their waste as possible, part of the waste problem can be solved. For recycling to be a success, however, it has to be easy to do, or convenient.

Examples of this include: doorstep collections where householders put out items for recycling in special bins or boxes, recycling bins on street corners and at shops. Recycling points that are placed in more remote locations are usually restricted to people who have cars. It is important that people do not have to drive out of their way to recycle their rubbish and in doing so waste petrol and add to harmful emissions in the atmosphere. Also, there needs to be a demand for the recycled items. There is no point in recycling vast quantities of glass or paper, for example, if there is no end use for them.

A highly successful recycling programme has been running in Curitiba, Brazil since 1989. The 'garbage that is not garbage' programme has been joined by 10,000 families. They each receive 2 kilograms of food for every 4 kilograms of recyclable rubbish they deliver to mobile recycling units. Approximately 60 tons of paper is recycled every day, which is like saving 1200 trees.

A materials recovery facility is a central collection point for household waste. The useful parts of the waste, including aluminium and other metals, card and plastic, are removed and recycled. The remainder may be burned to generate electricity, or taken to a landfill site.

Industrial waste

Turning raw materials into products makes waste. This waste includes that from both agricultural and manufacturing industries. Agricultural waste consists of things such as pesticides, empty pesticide containers, plastic wrapping, bags and sheets, packaging waste, old machinery, oil and waste veterinary medicines. Manufacturing waste depends on the technology used, the type of raw material processed, and how much of it is thrown away at the end of the process. Each stage of the production process generates a specific type of waste. In general, there are three groups of manufacturing waste:

- waste from extraction and transformation of raw materials, such as soil and rock in quarrying
- waste from manufacturing and production of goods (including building construction) such as leftover plastics, metals and unused mortar from building walls
- waste from distribution and consumption of manufactured goods, such as packaging, pallets on which goods are moved, lengths of plastic and wire.

There are ways of tackling this waste problem. Some involve governments making specific laws about waste, but others are voluntary schemes undertaken by individual companies to reduce, reuse and recycle their waste and to develop their business in a sustainable way.

There are official environmental standards that companies can meet. These standards show the public that the company cares for the environment and helps to gain the company a good reputation with their customers. For example, the international standard ISO14001 requires a company to establish an environmental policy and to consider how their products or services impact on the environment. Worldwide, around 89,000 companies have achieved this standard. There are several advantages to a company changing their business practices to meet this environmental standard, including an increase in efficiency, a reduction in the use of energy and raw materials, and the production of less waste.

Producer pays

Increasingly, laws are being passed around the world to make producers or manufacturers of products and packaging responsible for their recycling. This is often referred to as 'producer responsibility'. The laws encourage companies to make their products with the minimal use of raw materials, to produce products with longer life spans, and to recover and recycle the products that are thrown away by the consumer. The European Union has applied 'Extended Producer Responsibility' (EPR) to packaging, vehicles and electrical and electronic products. Surprisingly, the USA has no federal laws (laws that cover all states) concerned with producer responsibilities, although a number of states have laws, and some companies have voluntary schemes in place.

Green design

The term 'green design' describes the various techniques used when considering the environment at each of the design stages of a product or system. The aim of green design is to conserve or minimise any damage to the environment. All products have some environmental impact, but some use more resources, cause more pollution or generate more waste than others. Using green design helps to identify those that cause least damage. For example, a green design can be achieved by using products that contain recyclable materials and recycled content, and by using the least toxic materials and manufacturing processes. It is also important to minimise or remove any unnecessary parts and to ensure that the product can carry out its function for as long as possible. There are now more requirements for manufacturers to take back products, such as computer equipment, at the end of their life. This has encouraged manufacturers to consider designs that can be taken apart and recycled.

"Once companies realize that they are going to have to pay for waste management and recycling, they have an incentive to make less wasteful products and to design for recyclability by reducing the materials and parts used, particularly reducing the number of different plastics, labelling them, and designing fasteners for easy disassembly."

Spokesperson for a US-based environmental research organisation.

"Extended Producer Responsibilities (EPR) on packaging has become too complex in Europe."

Publisher, Recycling Laws International, USA

Having a working lunch is common today and office workers eat pre-packaged foods at their desks. This practice generates large quantities of waste in the form of plastic cups, paper serviettes, and card and plastic packing.

What are incinerators?

Incineration is a common way of disposing of waste. The waste, both household and industrial, is burned at high temperatures. The waste product is an ash that is disposed of in landfill sites. Incinerators provide a convenient way of getting rid of waste, but there are both advantages and disadvantages to their construction.

Incinerators are expensive to build, at approximately £228 million each. The most recent ones have very strict emission controls, using filters in their chimneys, and incorporate a waste-to-energy plant that generates electricity for local homes and businesses. In some areas of the world, incinerators play a central role in waste management. For example, on Long Island, New York, as much as 50 per cent of household waste is burned in 5 waste-to-energy incinerators. Often, it is more efficient to burn wastes such as mixed plastics, which are difficult to recycle.

Harmful emissions

There have been problems with emissions from incinerators. The Baldovie incinerator in Scotland, for example, had to be shut down because the emissions contained high levels of the toxic chemical dioxin, which came from burning PVC (a type of plastic). Sometimes the ash contains high levels of heavy metals such as mercury and lead. Removing PVC plastics from the waste could reduce the dioxin emission problem.

However, a major source of PVC is hospital waste and this needs to be incinerated for health reasons. Hospitals could be encouraged to work with reusable equipment rather than disposables and to purchase non-PVC alternatives, but these tend to be more expensive.

This incinerator in Hong Kong, with smoke pouring out of its chimneys, has been built close to a residential area. The emissions from the chimneys drift over the area.

Electricity from waste

Incineration does not solve the problem of waste. In fact it tends to encourage people to continue to produce waste because it can be burned. Waste-to-energy plants need waste with a high content of plastic, paper and organic matter. This is because these materials contain a lot of carbon, which releases heat when it is burned. The heat is used to generate electricity. Incinerators need a steady stream of waste to keep the generators going so tend to compete with local recycling schemes, with waste going to be burned instead of being recycled.

Recycling instead

As landfill sites fill up, the real alternative to incineration is recycling. In both developed and developing countries, recycling generates more jobs, less pollution and is more sustainable than incineration. In Europe and North America, there are a range of high-tech industries springing up that deal with making products from recycled materials, while in the developing world recycling projects are creating jobs for the poorest members of society. It must be remembered, however, that there is still an environmental cost to recycling, although it is much less than using raw materials.

Waste fact

Choosing to recycle, rather than burn, waste saves energy. Recycling paper saves three times the energy than that gained by burning, plastic five times and textiles six times.

"Landfilling is becoming more expensive and waste-to-energy plants have improved. It really requires a fresh look."

Member of an environmental research group

"Incineration is inconsistent with reduction, reuse and recycling because it relies on a steady, large quantity of mixed waste. It is a superficial solution that does not attack the root of the problem – we must waste less."

Ruth Grier, Government Minister for the Environment, Canada

All forms of waste disposal create jobs for people, but recycling schemes are labour-intensive and create far more jobs than a landfill operation. This can be important in countries where there are high levels of unemployment.

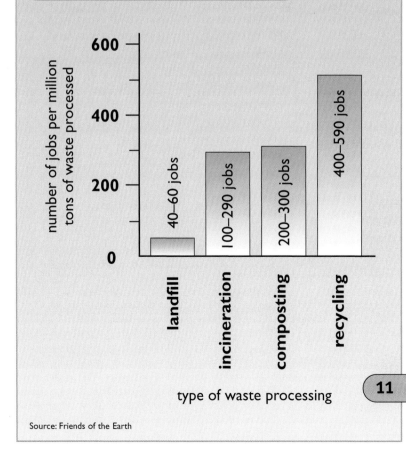

number of jobs per million tons of waste processed

- landfill: 40–60 jobs
- incineration: 100–290 jobs
- composting: 200–300 jobs
- recycling: 400–590 jobs

type of waste processing

Source: Friends of the Earth

Glass

The first glass dates back to 4000 BC when it was used to make jewellery. Since that time it has been used in a wide range of objects including containers for cooking and drinking. Today, glass is a very common material. It was one of the first materials to be recycled and now a large percentage of all glass bottles and containers are recycled.

Making glass

Glass was an expensive material until the 1800s when the mass-production of glass containers began. Today, the raw materials are more readily available so it is fairly cheap to make. Glass is made from three main ingredients: sand, soda ash and limestone. The ingredients are added together in a furnace and then heated until they melt. The molten glass is then poured into moulds or blown to make bottles or other containers. Glass making needs a source of heat, which is usually produced by burning fossil fuels.

Newly made bottles in this glassworks in France are automatically filled with liquid. France recycles just over 50 per cent of glass bottles, in particular the green glass used by the wine industry. Nine out of ten champagne bottles are made from recycled glass.

Reducing and reusing bottles

There are ways of reducing the amount of glass needed. Modern bottles, for example, are much lighter than in the past and this saves on manufacturing and transport costs. Just 5 years ago a small beer bottle weighed 260 grams, but this has now been reduced, by almost a third, to 170 grams.

Once a bottle has been used, it can either be reused or recycled. From an environmental point of view, it is much better to reuse a bottle than to recycle it. Less energy is used in the collection, cleaning and refilling of a bottle than is needed to recycle it.

During the 1950s and 1960s it was quite common to take bottles back to shops from where they would be collected and taken back to the factory. As the manufacturing plants became larger and began to supply bottles to further-away places, it became too costly to take the bottles back to the factory so this practice slowly died away. In the UK, milk is still delivered to some homes in bottles. The average milk bottle is used about twenty times. In the developing world, reusing glass bottles is more common and soft drinks and beer often come in glass bottles that are collected and returned to the factory.

Clear glass containers such as jam jars are frequently reused in homes for jam making and pickling amongst other things. However, a bottle or jar that is to be collected from homes or shops and reused many times has to be made from heavier, thicker glass, in order to withstand wear and tear. Because of this, more glass is used in its manufacture and more energy in its transportation. There are also the additional costs of collection, transportation and cleaning.

These crates, stacked in a street in Phalenksangu, in the Nepalese Himalayas, are full of empty soft drink bottles, which will be taken back to the factory for cleaning and refilling.

Recycling glass

The great thing about glass is that is can be recycled very easily, and this can happen over and over again without any loss of quality. It was the first material to be regularly recycled and today a large percentage of all glass is recycled. In Finland and Switzerland, for example, as much as 90 per cent of glass is recycled. Glass collected from factories and bottle banks is taken to recycling plants where it is monitored for purity – that is if it's all the same colour with no foil or caps – and crushed to make cullet. Then the cullet is mixed in with the other raw materials and melted.

Environmental benefits

Recycling has a number of environmental benefits. Firstly, cullet melts at a lower temperature than is needed to make glass from raw materials so this saves energy. Secondly, if this energy source was a fossil fuel, this reduces carbon dioxide emissions. Even after transport and processing, every ton of cullet melted saves 31 kilograms of carbon dioxide. It also reduces the need for raw materials that have to be taken from the ground. Limestone quarries can be located in attractive settings and often spoil the natural landscape. Recycling glass reduces the need to quarry for limestone and prevents this kind of damage.

Still thrown away

Despite the fact that glass is easy to recycle much of it still ends up in rubbish bins and in landfills. One large source of this glass is bottles from bars and nightclubs. These businesses sell large numbers of bottles each night and only a small percentage is recycled. Although the UK recycles more than 1 million tons of glass per year, glass still makes up 7 per cent of the average dustbin contents in the UK. In 2001 more than 2.5 million tons of glass ended up in UK landfills. Currently, UK households recycle just 34 per cent of container glass.

This Danish supermarket has a 'money back' machine. People drop a bottle in the top and receive a small payment in return. This money encourages people to recycle their bottles.

One problem with recycling glass is that it comes in different colours. When the different colours are mixed up, the recycled glass has a lower value because there are fewer uses. There is a shortage of clear glass, which is the most useful. In the UK much of the recycled glass is green glass from wine bottles. These bottles have been imported from other wine-producing countries and there is only a small market for recycled green glass in the UK. Usually the green glass cullet is exported back to the country it came from for recycling.

Case Study: Successful recycling in Switzerland

In Switzerland, 90 per cent of all glass bottles sold are recycled. In a few areas of the country this figure is as high as 93.8 per cent. Switzerland's amazingly high recycling figure has been achieved in a number of ways. Firstly, there are glass banks everywhere so that people do not have to travel to recycle their glass. There are collection points in shops, too. Switzerland is a very clean country with hardly any litter on the streets so recycling is also part of their national pride. At school, children are taught to respect their environment and they are encouraged to recycle. Children are taught rhymes to help them to remember to recycle.

New uses

Recycled glass can be used in a number of ways. The most common is to make new glass bottles and jars. In recent years, however, a number of new products that make use of recycled glass have appeared. These include the use of glass as decorative garden paving, in mosaics and jewellery. Glass can also be used as a filtrate to remove impurities from water. The construction industry is also a major user of recycled glass. They use it to make glasphalt, which is a type of road surface that contains 30 per cent recycled glass. Glasphalt can be made with all different types of glass mixed together.

At this recycling plant, this huge pile of empty glass bottles is ready to be recycled and made into new objects or containers.

15

Metals

Metals are materials with valuable properties. For example, steel is strong and long lasting, while lead is more flexible and can be bent into shape. These properties mean that metals are very useful, and there are few materials that can replace them. As developing countries become more industrialised, the use of metal increases. Currently, the industrial expansion of China and India is causing shortages of metals such as copper, iron and steel, which are all used in construction. This shortage is pushing up the cost of these essential metals. Reducing the world's use of metals will be difficult, so the emphasis has to be on reuse and recycling.

Extracting and recycling

Most metals are extracted from the ground as ores. Ores are the rocks that contain the metal. For example, aluminium occurs in an ore called bauxite, while mercury occurs in cinnabar. The ores contain other substances, for example, most iron ores contain sand, rock and silica, too. The metal ores have to be crushed and then processed to remove any impurities. This processing usually requires a lot of energy and generates considerable waste as well as pollutants such as sulphur dioxide, which is one of the gases responsible for acid rain. Iron ore, for example, is refined in a blast furnace and the waste products include slag, which is a mix of limestone and impurities from the iron ore, dust and gas.

Metal objects are easy to recycle. The metal is simply heated until it melts, and then moulded into a new shape. Metals can be recycled over and over again with no loss in quality. In fact, there is so much metal already in existence that it could be possible not to have to extract any more ore from the ground.

This huge quarry in the rainforest of Papua New Guinea digs out metal ores that contain copper and silver. The quarry is located on the side of a hill and it creates huge piles of waste. The high rainfall means that water carries silt into local streams and rivers.

Most of the valuable metals can be recycled including steel, copper, aluminium, lead, tin, zinc, gold, silver and platinum. Today, about 45 per cent of all steel and nearly 40 per cent of the world's copper come from recycled sources. However, some metals have to be recycled by specialist processors. For example, gold and platinum can be recovered from old electronic equipment such as computers, but the process is complex and hazardous to health as these metals are harmful if inhaled (as vapour) or if absorbed through the skin.

Why recycle?

There are several benefits of recycling metals. By not having to extract ores from the ground there can be fewer quarries. Quarries are not only unattractive to look at, but they also produce a lot of waste soil and rock. Often this waste is dumped in piles around the quarry. Large vehicles have to carry the ore from the quarry: creating dust and traffic problems, and using fuel. Recycling means fewer quarries and less air pollution. Ores are often transported long distances because some metal ores, such as bauxite, are found only in certain parts of the world. Bauxite is shipped from Australia to North America and Europe.

This man in Botswana is reusing aluminium cans as a building material to construct a wall. In the developing world the lack of resources can mean that people are more imaginative about what can be done with 'waste' materials.

This transportation can be avoided if metals are recycled. Metal ores have to be processed and this uses more energy and creates more waste than melting down and reusing metal.

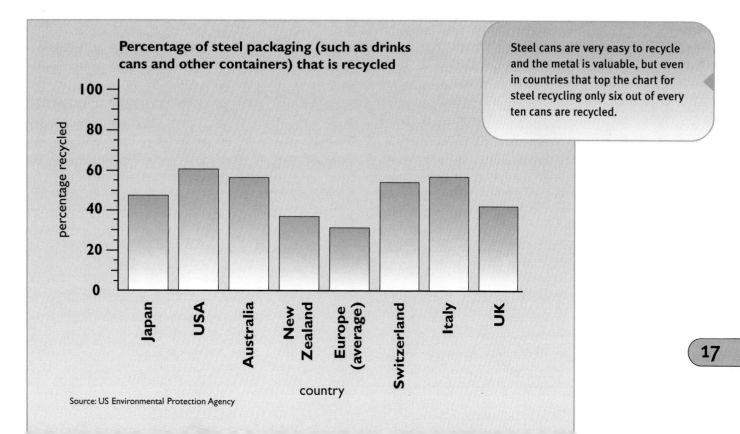

Percentage of steel packaging (such as drinks cans and other containers) that is recycled

Steel cans are very easy to recycle and the metal is valuable, but even in countries that top the chart for steel recycling only six out of every ten cans are recycled.

percentage recycled

country

Japan, USA, Australia, New Zealand, Europe (average), Switzerland, Italy, UK

Source: US Environmental Protection Agency

Using aluminium

Aluminium is a shiny, strong, malleable metal that can be rolled very thin. It is also lightweight so it is ideal for making items such as drink cans, aerosols, folding chairs and ladders. It is the preferred metal for drink cans as it keeps drinks fresh, cools quickly in the fridge and can be crushed and recycled. In 2001, more than 200 billion cans were sold around the world. To meet this demand, the current world production of refined aluminium is in excess of 18 million tons.

Making aluminium

Aluminium is obtained from bauxite ore. Bauxite is unsustainable, because one day it will run out. There are huge bauxite quarries in countries such as Australia and Jamaica. A lot of energy is needed to quarry the ore, transport it around the world, and then extract the pure metal. Making new aluminium objects from recycled aluminium is much easier. Aluminium is melted down and shaped into ingots. The ingots can be stored until needed. When they are heated, they can be rolled and shaped into new objects.

Case Study: Cash for cans

Aluminium is a valuable metal, so collecting cans is a great way for organisations and schools to raise money for charity. About 50,000 cans weigh 1 ton and when they are crushed they take up about 4 cubic metres. There is a network of companies across Europe, Australia and the USA that run 'buy back' centres where people can take their cans and swap them for cash. Two charities in the UK – Alupro and Tree Aid – have joined forces to sponsor tree planting in Burkina Faso, West Africa, with the money raised from recycling cans. The leader in aluminium can recycling is Brazil. In 2004, more than 16,000 schools, day care centres, and institutions in Brazil exchanged aluminium cans for more than 14,000 items, including electronic equipment, furniture, school kits and food baskets.

These children in Brazil have collected aluminium cans from a beach. The cans will be crushed and sold to a scrap merchant.

This process requires far less energy than making the metal from bauxite. Recycling means there are savings in transportation costs, pollution and quarrying. Worldwide, about 50 per cent of aluminium cans are recycled.

Reducing use of aluminium

There are ways of reducing the amount of aluminium being used. Today, empty aluminium cans weigh about 14 grams, which is about 30 per cent lighter than they were 25 years ago. This means that there are considerable savings made both in the amount of aluminium needed to make the cans and in transportation costs.

It's not just aluminium cans that can be recycled. A slightly different form of aluminium is used in cooking foil, bottle tops and baking and freezing trays and these are all good sources of aluminium. The recycled aluminium from these sources is used by the car manufacturing industry for casting engine blocks and cylinder heads. This aluminium is actually an alloy, which is a mix of at least two elements, one of which must be a metal. This changes the properties of the aluminium and it means that this aluminium must be kept separate from aluminium cans.

Aluminium facts

▶ Recycling 1 kilogram of aluminium saves up to 8 kilograms of bauxite, 4 kilograms of chemical products and 14 kilowatt-hours of electricity compared with extracting the metal from bauxite.

▶ Twenty recycled aluminium cans can be made with the energy it takes to make one can from raw materials.

▶ Aluminium transfers heat 2.4 times faster than iron. This, combined with the fact that very thin sheets can be produced, means that heat is lost and gained through aluminium very quickly. It is ideal for cooking and as a cold drink container.

▶ It's easy to tell a steel can from an aluminium can: a magnet will stick to the steel can, but drop off the aluminium one.

Source: Waste Watch

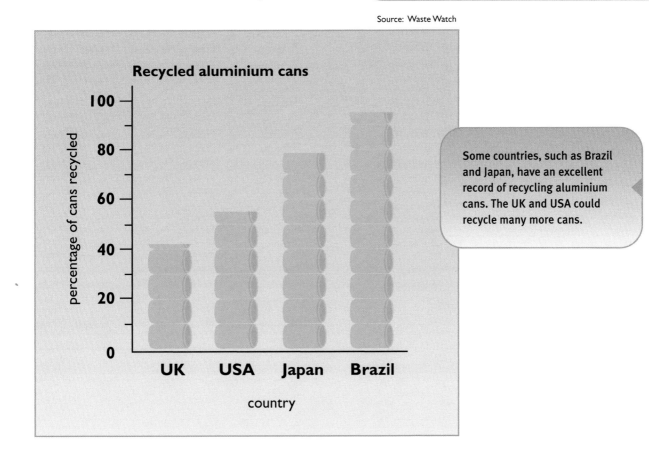

Some countries, such as Brazil and Japan, have an excellent record of recycling aluminium cans. The UK and USA could recycle many more cans.

Plastics, textiles and paper

Plastics, textiles and paper are all incredibly useful materials. These materials are all around us – in plastic containers, our clothes, newspapers and magazines. Some of these materials are sustainable if used properly, some can be recycled and others reused.

Plastics

Plastic is extremely versatile and vast quantities of it are manufactured each year. It is a popular packaging material because it is lightweight, but strong, and can be clear so that consumers can see the contents. Although it is useful, a lot of plastic ends up in landfill sites once it has been thrown away. It does not weigh as much as other forms of waste, but it is bulky and can take hundreds of years to break down, if at all.

Using plastic

There are pros and cons to using plastics. The use of plastic can help to conserve other resources. Plastics are lightweight, long lasting and can be shaped easily. These features enable manufacturers to do more with less material. This is known as source reduction. Source reduction is the process by which a package or product is made using fewer resources, creating less pollution and using fewer ingredients. Source reduction can also involve an improvement in the functionality and durability of a product.

These Bangladeshi women and their children are paid to sort plastic bottles into different colours and types at a recycling centre in Dhaka, Bangladesh.

Since plastic is lightweight it can be used to make large containers that would be too heavy for consumers if they were made from glass. Also, it requires less fuel to move the containers from the factory to the shop. Plastics can take up less space, too. Paper bags take up seven times more space than the same number of plastic bags. So, one lorry load of plastic bags would mean seven lorries if the bags were made of paper. Although these features help the environment, it must be remembered that not all plastics are easy to recycle, which means they end up in landfills or incinerators.

Saving energy?

There is no doubt that plastics can save energy. Studies in the USA looked at the energy required to manufacture, use and dispose of common packaging items, such as bottles, tubs and wraps, and compared this with the most likely non-plastic alternatives. By using plastic rather than the alternatives, product manufacturers in the USA would save enough energy each year to power a city of 1 million homes for more than 3 years. However, plastics are manufactured from fossil fuels, especially oil. Fossil fuels are unsustainable resources that are quickly being depleted. In addition, fossil fuels release carbon dioxide when they are burned and this carbon dioxide is contributing to global warming. The way forward may be to make plastics from natural oils obtained from plants such as oil seed rape. Oil seed rape and other oil producing crops could be grown on a much larger scale, but it would need governments to encourage farmers to grow these crops and to invest in new equipment.

Plastic facts

▶ Plastic production uses 8 per cent of the world's oil. About 4 per cent of this oil is used as a raw material and 4 per cent as an energy source for the manufacturing process.

▶ In India, use of plastic is 2 kilograms per person per year. In European countries it is 60 kilograms per person per year, and in the USA it is 80 kilograms per person per year.

▶ In India, cows are considered to be sacred animals and they are allowed to roam freely. Unfortunately, as many as 100 cows die each day after eating plastic bags that they find littering the ground. Plastic litter is a problem in South Africa, too, where studies showed 90 per cent of blue petrel chicks on Marion Island (off the coast of South Africa) had plastic in their stomachs, fed to them by their parents.

Plastic bags can be carried by the wind and get trapped on trees and fences. As well as being unsightly, it can also be a threat to wildlife. This fallow deer has plastic caught on its antlers.

21

Reducing and reusing plastics

The best way to tackle the problem of plastic waste is to reduce the amount of waste that is produced. This could be achieved in a number of ways. Manufacturers and shops could avoid using unnecessary packaging. Shoppers could reuse heavy plastic bags to carry their shopping, rather than pick up a new bag each time they buy something. Plastic bottles can be reused or put to some other use instead of being thrown away. There is a market for quality second-hand plastic containers that can be put to a new use, for example large, heavy-duty plastic containers can be reused as water butts or feed containers for livestock. Some of the quality plastic components in cars can be removed and reused.

Recycling plastic

Plastics can be quite difficult to recycle, because many plastic items are made up of several different types of plastic. The different types have to be separated before they can be recycled. Plastic bottles can be recycled because they are made from one of only three types of plastic and this can be identified easily. Some plastic packaging is made from blended plastic, which cannot be identified so easily. The blended plastic is usually burned in an incinerator rather than being placed in a landfill. Different types of plastic can be identified from the number or code that appears on them inside a triangular recycling symbol. However, the presence of this code does not always mean that the item can be recycled easily.

These plastic bottles are being reused as mini cloches. These are used to protect young plants from being killed off by bad weather, such as frost, before they have the chance to develop. This is just one example of how plastic can be reused – can you think of any others?

The plastic bottles and containers are sorted, cleaned and then shredded to form granules. These granules are melted down and moulded into a new object. There is an increasing range of recycled plastic objects including plastic plant pots, wellington boots, garden decking and benches. Plastic bottles made from PET (see table below) are particularly useful because the plastic can be used to make egg boxes, new bottles, fibre filling for duvets and anoraks, carpets, rugs, and even fleece jackets. PVC is used to make drainage pipes and electrical fittings. Currently, the demand for recycled plastic in many countries is greater than the supply, so there is plenty of reason for people to recycle more.

All sorts of amazing products can be made from recycled plastic bottles, including fleece jackets! It takes just 25 2-litre fizzy drink bottles to make an adult-size fleece jacket.

Different types of plastics

Symbol	Type of plastic	Properties	Use
PET	polyethylene terephthalate	rigid, clear or green	fizzy drink bottles
PVC	polyvinyl chloride	semi-rigid, glossy	squash and mineral water bottles
HDPE	high density polyethylene	semi-rigid	milk bottles and fabric conditioner bottles
LD PE	low density polyethylene	flexible	bread bags, plastic carriers
PP	polypropylene	semi-rigid	margarine tubs, screw top lids
PS	polystyrene	brittle and glossy	takeaway packaging, foam cups
OTHER	multilayer plastics	squeezable	ketchup and syrup bottles

Textiles

Every day, we use a wide range of textiles including curtains, carpets and clothes. Many of these are made from fibres such as cotton, wool, linen and sisal. All of these textiles can be recycled, but many just get thrown away and end up on landfills.

Reusing textiles

One of the main problems today is the number of cheap clothes that are being sold. Low prices mean that people are more likely to throw old clothes away and buy new ones rather than alter and reuse them. However, there is a second-hand market for more expensive designer clothing and items such as carpets and curtains. These textiles are sold in specialist second-hand shops.

Efficient recycling

Textiles are very efficient to recycle because textile reprocessors are able to recycle as much as 93 per cent of textiles without producing any harmful by-products or wastes. When the textiles arrive at the recycling centre they are identified, graded and sorted. This is a highly skilled job because the workers have to be able to identify a type of cloth or textile in seconds. Any good quality clothing and shoes are removed and sent to charity shops or exported to developing countries. For example, trainers with little wear are sent to countries such as Bangladesh where goods of such quality are often far too expensive or unavailable. This leaves the worn or damaged textiles, which can be cut and made into industrial wiping cloths. Any textiles that are unsuitable for making into cloths are used for other products. For example, woollen or cotton clothes can be unravelled and the threads woven into new clothes, blankets or used for filling mattresses. Some of these reclaimed fibres may be used by specialist companies to make new designer clothes.

TRAID (Textile Recycling for Aid and International Development) is one organization that makes new, recycled clothes out of unwanted clothes that have been donated to them. The new clothes are fashionable, as well as environmentally friendly, and the money raised from selling them goes to fund international projects for sustainability.

Case Study: The nappy story

A baby will have approximately 2000 nappy changes a year and use up to 6000 disposable nappies until potty trained. In a household with a baby, disposable nappies can make up 50 per cent of the household's waste. Once in a landfill, disposable nappies swell up in the rain. Consequently, they make up between 2 and 8 per cent of landfill volume.

A disposable nappy is made up mostly of plastic, with some wood fibres. After it has been used it is usually wrapped in a plastic bag and thrown away. A used nappy may be full of human sewage too, so dumping all this untreated sewage in landfills is not very healthy. It would be far better if the content of the nappy were put into the sewage system to be treated properly. Disposable nappies are quite expensive, too. In some countries, such as New Zealand, disposable nappies are imported and this has further environmental costs of transportation.

So what are the alternatives? The answer is 'real' nappies made from natural fibres such as cotton. A real nappy can be washed and reused many times over. One argument against the real nappy is that they are not as easy to use and they are not waterproof. However, the latest real nappies look very similar to disposable ones as they are shaped and come with a waterproof outer cover that can also be washed. Since they are reused, these nappies only have to be purchased once. However, they do have to be washed at high temperatures and so there is an environmental cost from the washing machine, which will use electricity, water and detergents.

Disposable nappies such as this one may seem harmless, but are a huge contributor to the waste problem.

Paper

Most paper is made from a sustainable source – trees that can be harvested, and replanted. So long as more trees are planted than are cut down, the process is sustainable. Fast-growing trees, such as spruce, fir and eucalyptus, are planted for paper production.

Making paper

Making paper starts with wood chips from the harvested trees. The chips are placed in pulp digesters where they are broken up by steam and chemicals into a pulp of fibres and other components of wood. These extra components, such as resin and lignin, are removed by further processing, leaving a pulp of pure fibres. The pulp is mixed with water and chemicals to form a mushy mix that is spread out and rolled to make paper.

If you look at paper with a microscope you will see that it is made of long fibres. Better quality papers have longer fibres. Paper is a relatively straightforward material to recycle because old paper can be mixed in with the pulp. Each time paper is recycled, however, the fibres get shorter and this reduces the quality of the recycled paper. The lowest grade paper is used for newspapers.

Saving paper

Each year, large volumes of paper waste end up in landfills, mostly in the form of packaging and printed materials. Some of this will be contaminated with food and glue and therefore it cannot be recycled. One way to reduce the amount of paper in landfills is to reduce the amount of paper that is used and thrown away. Paper can be saved in all sorts of ways, for example, by not printing out unnecessary sheets of paper from a computer, using scrap paper as a note pad and using both sides of a sheet of paper before throwing it away. Businesses can reduce the paper they use by sending emails rather than faxes and letters, and sending some documents and reports electronically rather than printing them out. White office paper should be kept separate from coloured or glossy paper when recycling.

At the end of the paper making process, the paper is passed through a series of heated rollers that press and dry it. Finally, it is turned on to a huge roll and moved to the cutting room.

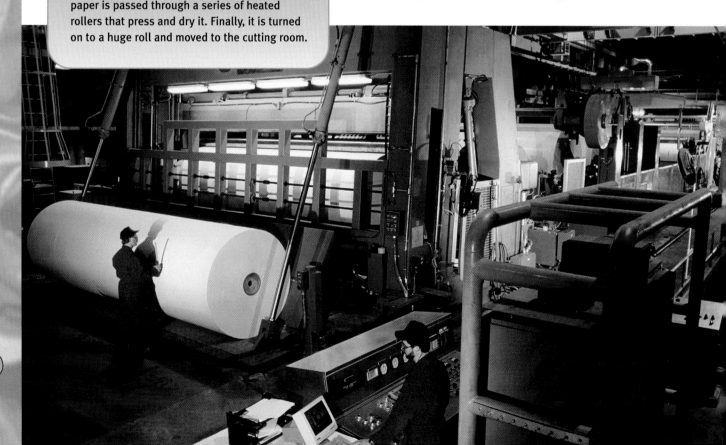

Shredded newspaper can be blown into cavity walls to make an efficient and renewable source of insulation.

Recycling paper

If paper has to be thrown away, it is important to make sure that it is recycled. Usually, the different types of paper, for example, newsprint, magazines, cardboard and office paper, are kept separate because each type has a different length of fibre. Waste paper does not have to be recycled into new paper. Paper can be shredded and used for animal bedding or building insulation.

Some types of paper and card are difficult to recycle, especially waxed corrugated cardboard containers used for food. However, this can be composted. The paper and card is shredded and placed in large compost bins where worms, fungi and bacteria break it down. The resulting compost can be sold for use in gardens.

Paper facts

▶ In the USA, paper recycling averages 154 kilograms a year for every person. This has increased from 106 kilograms per person per year in 1990.

▶ In the UK, newsprint is made from 75 per cent recovered fibres, although this figure varies from year to year.

▶ In 1989, there was only one mill in Canada capable of making newsprint with recycled content. Today, there are more than 25 such mills out of 150.

Cars and e-waste

The market for consumer goods is huge and is growing rapidly. In the modern world, people do not keep items such as cars, televisions, videos, phones or computers for very long. New models with enhanced features continue to appear and there is a huge demand to have the latest gadget or mobile phone. It is often costly or impossible to repair modern electrical goods, so it can be cheaper to buy new products. The increasing number of consumer goods being sold is producing large volumes of waste in the form of 'old models'. Much of this waste has to be specially treated.

Cars

The number of cars in the world is increasing, particularly in countries such as China and India. In 1990 there were just 1 million cars on Chinese roads, but by 2004 this had risen to 12 million. A further increase of 2.4 million new cars occurred in 2005. If these increases continue there could be a staggering 140 million cars by 2020.

Cars have considerable environmental impact. Firstly, car manufacturing uses a lot of raw materials such as steel and aluminium, as well as energy. Secondly, new cars may be transported around the world. While they are being driven, cars use energy and produce pollutants. Finally, at the end of a car's life it is scrapped. The life span of a car has got shorter. In the past, cars would be kept for twenty years or more, now it is common for a car to be scrapped after just ten years or so, especially those which have been involved in accidents.

Although car ownership is still relatively uncommon in rural areas of China, in cities such as Beijing traffic congestion is becoming a problem. If car ownership continues to grow in China there will be damaging consequences for the environment.

At recycling centres like this one in Japan, the useful parts of cars are removed and reused before the bodywork is crushed and recycled.

Recycling cars

As much as 75 per cent of a car can be recycled, and there is no reason why this figure cannot reach 95 per cent. It used to be just the metal frame of a car that was saved, but modern scrapyards are far more organised. Now, all the useable parts of a car are removed and sold as spare parts. This includes engine parts, plastics and even the interior light bulbs. Strict rules in many countries require old cars to be taken to specific sites where they can be scrapped and in some cases the car owner has to obtain a certificate of scrapping to prove that the car was not just dumped. Car manufacturers are under greater obligation to be responsible for the recycling of old cars, so they are beginning to change car design in order to make recycling much easier.

Leaving the car behind

Recycling old cars does not really solve the problem of more cars being manufactured and the increasing use of petrol to fuel them. As traffic congestion around the world gets worse, governments are looking for ways of persuading people to leave their cars behind and use public transport instead. Some of the measures being taken to encourage drivers include:

- road or congestion charges
- high taxes on car purchases, ownership and fuel
- cheaper public transport.

In Beijing, China, the rise in private car ownership is creating smog and severe traffic congestion, so the city is introducing measures such as a fuel tax, high parking charges and tighter regulations on exhaust emissions.

"If each Chinese family has two cars like US families, then the cars needed by China, something like 600 million vehicles, will exceed all the cars in the world combined. That would be the greatest disaster for mankind."

Chinese environmentalist (Liang Congjie)

E-waste

Advances in technology have brought with them a new type of waste – electrical and electronic waste, or 'e-waste'. This type of waste barely existed twenty years ago. Now, e-waste represents the biggest and fastest-growing manufacturing waste. As products are continually invented and updated the life of the old ones gets shorter, and the waste problem gets larger.

Not only is there a large quantity of e-waste, but also it is difficult to recycle because the equipment itself is made up of many different materials. The percentage composition varies, too. For example, a television contains about 6 per cent metal and 50 per cent glass while a cooker is 89 per cent metal and only 6 per cent glass. There are other materials, too, such as plastics, ceramics and heavy metals.

The main component of e-waste comes from large household appliances, such as fridges, freezers and washing machines, known as 'white goods'. They make up just under half of the total. The next largest component is I.T. equipment at 39 per cent, most of which is computers. Recently there has been an increase in the number of televisions and computer monitors being thrown away due to the arrival of new plasma and flat panel screens.

Recycling computers

Millions of computers are thrown away each year and you would think that much of this waste could be recycled. Unfortunately, this is not the case, as just 50 per cent of a computer is recycled and the rest is dumped. The major problem with computers is that they contain toxic heavy metals such as lead, mercury and cadmium. A computer can contain as much as 2 kilograms of lead and this is difficult to dispose of safely. In addition, much of the plastic in a computer contains flame retardant, which makes it difficult to recycle.

These mobile phones may only be a few years old, but already they are on the rubbish heap. Smaller, lighter phones as well as those with built-in cameras and MP3 players have taken the place of these old phones.

Most developed countries have strict rules regarding the disposal of computers because of the toxic metals they contain. This makes computer recycling very expensive. Some companies avoid the problem by shipping old computers to poorer countries. There, local people who are desperate to earn money take the computers to pieces. It is not uncommon to find entire communities, including children, earning their living by scavenging metals, glass and plastic from old computers. To extract a small quantity of gold, the capacitors have to be melted down over a charcoal fire. The plastic on the wires is burned in barrels to expose the valuable copper wires. The total value of the metals in a computer is about £3. The people who do this are risking their health because the burning plastic releases dioxins and other toxic gases into the air. The rest of the computer is worthless, so it is usually dumped near by where the remaining heavy metals contaminate the ground.

Case Study: Computers for the developing world

In today's world, computers are common and they have become a vital piece of equipment in schools, hospitals, offices and shops. They are also becoming more numerous in the developing world where more people are gaining access to the Internet. There are several charities, such as Computer Aid, which supply computers to people in the developing world. They take old computers from individuals and companies, repair and update them, then send them to schools and other organisations. This way, the life of the computer can be extended, which is more environmentally friendly than recycling. There can be problems, however. These refurbished computers can go wrong and when this happens, there is little technical support and so the computer often ends up on the scrap heap.

Facts about e-waste

▶ The manufacture of a new computer and monitor uses around 240 kilograms of fossil fuels, 22 kilograms of chemicals and 1500 litres of water.

▶ About 230 grams of gold can be recovered from 1 ton of old mobile phones.

▶ Discarded monitors and televisions are probably the largest sources of lead in landfills. The cathode ray tube found in most computer monitors and television screens contain 2 to 3 kilograms of lead, mostly embedded in glass.

These old computers in Australia are ready to be auctioned. Most of these computers will be bought for schoolchildren, or by college students.

These old fridges are waiting to be recycled. The coolant is drained out, filtered and reused, the insulating foam is removed, the oil drained for recycling and the metal making up the body of the fridge shredded and recycled.

Fridges, freezers and CFCs

Today, most homes in the developed world have a refrigerator and probably a freezer. These electrical appliances were relatively rare in developing countries, but now ownership is increasing worldwide. Refrigerators need a coolant to carry the heat from the refrigerator so that the inside stays cool. In the past, a chemical called CFC (chlorofluorocarbon) was used.

CFCs and ozone

For 50 years or so, CFCs were considered to be miracle chemicals. They were excellent coolants and solvents and they were used in aerosols, cleaning products and in refrigerators and freezers. However, once CFCs are released into the air, they destroy ozone molecules. Ozone is found in a layer high in the atmosphere where it has an important role in stopping harmful ultraviolet light in sunlight from reaching the ground. During the 1980s it was noticed that, particularly above the Antarctic, CFCs and other chemicals were depleting the ozone layer. Countries in the southern hemisphere, such as Australia and Chile, reported higher levels of ultraviolet light, which has led to more cases of skin cancer and eye cataracts. CFC is also a potent greenhouse gas. Each molecule of CFC has the same effect as several thousand carbon dioxide molecules. This means that a slight increase in the concentration of CFC in the atmosphere can cause a lot more heat to be trapped, resulting in the rise of global temperatures.

Government action

Global concern over the damage being caused by CFCs led to most countries signing the Montreal Protocol in 1987, which was an agreement to phase out the production of CFCs and closely related ozone-destroying chemicals. A few years later, CFC production was completely banned and no more CFCs were used as coolants. However, there were many millions of refrigerators and freezers containing CFCs already in existence, and these needed to be disposed of carefully to prevent the escape of CFCs into the atmosphere. In 2001, therefore, the European Union required CFCs and related chemicals to be removed from refrigeration equipment before it could be scrapped. This involves draining the cooling system and removing all the insulating foam.

Reusing fridges and freezers

One way to reduce the number of fridges and freezers being scrapped is to remove the CFCs from old refrigerators and freezers and then restore them to working order using new, CFC-free alternatives. In many countries there are organisations that train young people to refurbish old appliances. Sometimes old refrigerators and freezers containing CFCs are shipped to developing countries for resale. This is not always a good idea, however, because when this equipment finally stops working it may be abandoned: allowing the coolant to escape.

CFCs

Since 1987, more than 150 countries have signed the Montreal Protocol, which called for a phased reduction in the release of CFCs. In January 1996 a complete ban on CFCs came into effect. Even with this ban, CFCs will continue to accumulate in the atmosphere for another decade. It may take until the middle of the next century for ozone levels in the Antarctic to return to the levels of the 1970s.

These second-hand fridges are for sale in Serrekunda, The Gambia. They have been bought in from European countries and may contain harmful CFCs.

Mobile phones

The number of mobile phones worldwide is rapidly increasing, even in remote parts of Africa. At the same time, the production of phones with new features, such as built-in cameras and MP3 players, are persuading many people in the developed world to replace their mobile phone once a year. Sometimes people have to change their phone when they change providers. Not surprisingly, there are millions of discarded mobile phones making up about 1 to 2 per cent of e-waste. This may seem a small amount, but phones contain toxic chemicals such as arsenic, cadmium, antimony, beryllium, copper, nickel and mercury.

These chemicals are used in the manufacture of components such as the rechargeable battery and the LCD display. Therefore, mobile phones can contaminate the environment if they are not disposed of carefully. There are now schemes where shops collect old phones and donate the money raised from their recycling to charity. Phones are refurbished and sold to countries where the latest technology is not so important to consumers. Also, most of the mobile phone manufacturers have signed an international agreement to develop environmentally sound ways of dealing with end-of-life phones.

Mobile phone facts

▶ Each year, an estimated 130 million mobile phones end up in landfills or incinerators in the USA. In the UK about 15 million are thrown away in a year. In addition, there are probably hundreds of millions of old mobile phones lying in drawers and cupboards around the world.

▶ National phone companies in Europe and North America have joined up with charities to make a donation of between £1 and £50 for every mobile they receive. For example, 10,000 recycled mobile phones can pay for a guide dog for life.

Mobile phones are used around the world, and sometimes in unexpected places. This man in Botswana, for example, is busy talking on a mobile phone.

Reducing e-waste

As with other materials, it is possible to reduce the amount of e-waste. It would not be necessary to replace a computer so frequently if it was possible to upgrade the computer chips and repairs were easy to carry out. Computer designers could consider ways of reducing the number of cables and boxes that are attached to a computer and to concentrate on designing computers that have built-in accessories, which would reduce the use of raw materials.

Computers use a lot of consumable items such as printer cartridges. Most inkjet printer manufacturers design their cartridges so that they cannot be refilled, which means that the consumer has to buy new ones. Inkjet cartridges could be refilled easily and this would reduce waste. Other cartridges cannot be refilled and these have to be returned to the manufacturer. Usually, the packaging of a new cartridge contains a prepaid label so that the cartridge can be returned for recycling in the box that came with the replacement cartridge. Toner cartridges, for example, can be returned to a factory where they are completely dismantled and cleaned, any worn parts replaced, and the drum either re-coated or replaced. They are then refilled with fresh toner.

There are now laws in the European Union, known as the Waste Electrical and Electronic Equipment Directive (WEEE Directive), that are changing the way manufacturers deal with e-waste. As with packaging and other forms of waste, it is now the responsibility of the companies that manufacture or import electrical products to take back the products at the end of their 'life'. These companies are required to have collection points where users can return their old products free of charge.

"I talk to a lot of people who say they just want to make phone calls. They don't want to get email or download ringers or take photos. They don't need a new phone."

Spokesperson for the Wireless Consumer Alliance

"This new program encourages the recycling of mobile devices known to contain toxic materials, and therefore ultimately helps protects the environment. At the same time, it has the added benefit of raising money for worthy organizations."

Spokesperson for a mobile phone recycling company

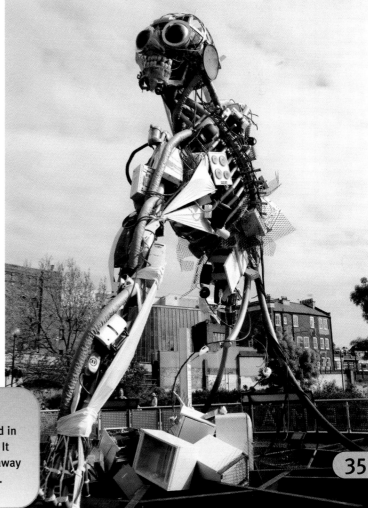

The WEEE man is a huge robotic figure made up of scrap electrical and electronic equipment, displayed in the UK. It weighs 3.3 tons and stands 7 metres tall. It represents the average amount of e-waste thrown away by a person in the developed world in their lifetime.

Waste and the developing world

In most developing countries, especially those in Africa, there is more reuse and recycling than in the developed world. In part, this is due to different ideas and cultures. Also, there is more poverty so people cannot afford to throw away and replace old goods if there is any way of reusing them.

Urban versus rural

Cities in many developing countries are usually large sprawling places. Often there are extensive areas of very poor housing and squatter camps where people have no services such as electricity, water and sewerage. There is little waste collection and there are large open dumps where rubbish is burned. Waste is often a big city problem. In rural areas there tends to be less waste and much of it is organic waste, such as food and sewage, which can be composted.

These people are picking over the rubbish in a huge waste tip in Manila, in the Philippines. A few are wearing gloves, but most have no protection on their hands or legs.

This young boy in South Africa is playing with a toy made from old wires and plastic wheels.

Waste scavengers

In the cities of Asia, Africa, Central and South America, many people make a living by sorting through huge waste dumps. They are called waste scavengers or rag pickers. They tend to be people who have moved to the city from the countryside looking for jobs, and are most often women and children. These people experience very dangerous working conditions and handle hazardous waste without physical protection. For example, many work without gloves or thick-soled shoes. However, their role is very important because they recycle a significant proportion of the waste. This reduces the amount of waste, increases recycling and creates jobs and wealth. The valuable job carried out by these people has been recognised in some cities and they are now beginning to get better pay and working conditions. In countries such as Columbia, Brazil and Argentina, waste scavengers are grouping together to form co-operatives in order to get a better price for the materials they collect.

Many of the items collected by waste scavengers are made into new goods that are then sold on. The range of goods that can be made from waste is incredibly varied. Oil cans are made into lamps, wire and small wheels can be shaped into toy cars for children, metal containers are flattened and used as a building material to make new homes.

The life of a waste scavenger

▶ Two per cent of the people who live in cities in the developing world make their living by scavenging on waste tips.

▶ In Mexico City, the life expectancy of a waste scavenger is 39 years compared with 67 years for the rest of the population.

Problem tyres

In many parts of the developing world, such as India, Pakistan and Southern Africa, old tyres are a massive problem. Sometimes these tyres are disposed of by being burned, which causes air pollution. Often the tyres are just dumped by roadsides or in the countryside where they trap pools of water. Malaria is a disease found in many developing countries and the mosquitoes that carry malaria can breed in these small tyre pools.

Fortunately the recycling of tyres has improved and tyres are becoming too valuable to throw away. Small businesses are springing up to collect, reuse or recycle tyres and this is creating new jobs. One way to extend the life of a tyre is to retread it. Tyres are discarded because the treads have been worn down and the tyre no longer grips the road. Old treads can be removed and new ones stuck on to the tyre. Some of the heavier tyres for lorries can be retreaded three to six times.

Alternatively, whole tyres can be reused as tree guards, plant pots, and even crash barriers on roads. Tyres can also be taken apart and put to various uses. For example, in Karachi, Pakistan tyre collectors remove the treads and cut them into thin strips to cover the wheels of donkey carts. The walls of tyres can be cut and shaped using simple tools into items such as soles of shoes, slippers, car windscreen washers and bike pedals. The bits of rubber can be broken into 'crumbs' that can be put to low grade uses such as rubber flooring, noise and vibration insulation, roof tiles, road surfacing and so on.

Old tyres can cause serious pollution if they are dumped or burned. It is much better for the environment if the tyres are reused or recycled in some way. These sandals for sale at Mahoney market Tigray, Ethiopia, for example, have been made using the rubber from old tyres.

Case Study: BMW and the Plastics Federation in South Africa

The German car manufacturer, BMW, has set up plastic recycling schemes in South Africa. During the manufacture of cars, lots of small bits of plastic are produced that could be recycled. However, the bits are in different colours, sizes and types of plastic, which means they need to be sorted first. BMW has joined up with the Plastics Federation of South Africa to train jobless people to sort the plastics into different types to sell on to recycling companies.

The scheme has proved to be so successful that it has been expanded to include the plastic waste from local schools. Plastic recycling has created many jobs and educated school children about the importance of waste management. More recently, BMW has sponsored green cages – recycling points in towns – where the public can take their plastic. All the plastic waste is taken to central collection points in BMW factories for baling, weighing and storing.

Dumping waste

There is a growing problem of richer countries disposing of their waste in poorer countries. There are strict rules regarding the disposal of waste in countries of the European Union, North America and Oceania and so some businesses find it is cheaper to export their waste to countries where the rules are less strict. For example, computers and printer cartridges are exported to China where unprotected workers break them up and retrieve the useful bits, exposing themselves to hazardous chemicals.

In recent years, many pesticides have been banned because they are too dangerous to use. When this happens, manufacturers have to destroy any stocks that they have. It is often cheaper, however, to ship the pesticides to poorer countries, especially those in Africa. Today there are huge stockpiles of dangerous pesticides, some of which were dumped as long as 40 years ago. They include harmful chemicals such as DDT, aldrin, dieldrin and chlordane. These countries are unable to dispose of the pesticides safely, so the stockpiles remain.

In Dhaka, Bangladesh, this nine-year-old girl works 7 days a week recycling batteries. She knocks open batteries with a hammer to recover the coil. Without any proper safety equipment, this job is a highly polluting and possibly cancer-causing activity.

Organic waste

One of the simplest ways of dealing with organic waste such as vegetable scraps from the kitchen and plant waste from the garden is to put it on a compost heap. Here, the waste is broken down naturally by worms, slugs, snails and micro-organisms such as bacteria and fungi. The resulting material can then be put back into the garden as a natural fertiliser for the soil. Animals produce a lot of waste in the form of dung and this can be an incredibly useful fuel. In many developing countries cow dung is collected and shaped into flat rounds and sun dried. Then the dung can be burned to provide heat for cooking.

Biogas

Biogas is a mix of gases including methane that can be burned for cooking, and to provide electricity. It is an important source of sustainable fuel. It is made from the organic wastes of animals and people as well as waste food. The organic waste is tipped into an underground container where the materials rot down and release gas, which is then collected. The waste slurry left in the pit is removed and used as a fertiliser on crops. Biogas digesters do not smell and are a hygienic way of using the wastes. Also, five times more energy is obtained from the waste using a biogas digester than by burning an equivalent quantity of animal dung.

This biodigester provides electricity for a whole school of children. The waste is put into the underground chamber (bottom left) where it breaks down and produces biogas. This is piped away and used as fuel to generate electricity for lighting and running school equipment.

Biogas has other benefits. It has created jobs for the women who collect the dung and other wastes, and who sell the slurry as fertiliser, and for men who build and maintain the digesters. Many remote villages were without electricity before the arrival of biogas. Now, the electricity generated using biogas can power many rural businesses. There are environmental benefits, too. Biogas has replaced firewood as the main source of fuel, so the forests are being conserved. Also, women have more time. Before, they would have spent many hours each day collecting firewood. Biogas is a much cleaner fuel to burn than either dung or wood, so there is less air pollution.

Biogas on a larger scale

In 1981, the Indian government started a scheme to install biogas digesters in the rural parts of the country. Now there are more than 2 million, most of which supply biogas to just one household. There are also several thousand larger plants that supply whole villages. It is only recently that the developed world has recognised the potential of animal wastes and biogas. Large-scale biogas digesters using agricultural waste have been built in countries such as the Netherlands, while there are dung-burning power stations in the UK and USA.

Vermiculture

Another way to break down organic household waste is to use worms. Worms are decomposers: animals that feed on organic matter and in doing so help to break it down and release nutrients back into the soil to be used by plants. Vermiculture (using worms) is very popular in Japan where more than 3000 million tons of earthworms are imported each year for vermiculture projects.

These small, red worms are used in vermiculture because they grow quickly and eat a lot of organic matter.

Case Study: Baobab fish farm, Kenya

Fish is an important source of protein in many developing countries. Fish such as tilapia can be bred in fish farms to provide a regular supply of food for local people. One such farm is Baobab fish farm in Kenya. The fish need a constant supply of clean water, but water is often in short supply. Baobab farm has found a way of cleaning the water so it can be recycled back into the fish ponds.

The waste water from the fish ponds is full of nutrients that are needed by plants so it is channelled to a series of beds where water-loving crops such as rice are grown. The plant roots take up the nutrients. The water that drains out of the crop beds is clean enough to be used in the fish pools again. This way water is recycled and the crops are fertilised by a waste product. More than 90,000 people visit Baobab fish farm each year and farmers in many parts of East Africa have set up similar sustainable systems, which are ideal for small farmers and villages.

Looking to the future

The world cannot continue to use raw materials and produce waste at the current rates. In general, people living in cities produce twice as much waste as people living in the country, mostly due to their dependence on pre-packed goods. Two-thirds of the world's population live in cities and this number is growing rapidly, so the waste problem is going to get even worse. Many of the raw materials come from unsustainable sources while the wastes may take many years to break down and may even produce toxic by-products. Landfill sites are filling up. It is essential, therefore, that the world addresses this problem and finds ways of reducing, reusing and recycling waste. The waste problem cannot be solved overnight and it will need to be approached in many different ways.

Zero waste

Today, most manufacturers produce goods in a way that is described as 'cradle-to-grave'. This involves the manufacture of a product from raw materials, the product's use and final disposal. A more sustainable approach is called the 'cradle-to-cradle' system. This system involves manufacturers working together. The waste products of one manufacturer become the raw materials of another, eliminating as much waste as possible. This is more like the cycles found in the natural world: where the wastes of one organism are broken down and used by other organisms.

Using sustainable materials

Another way forward would be greater use of sustainable sources for making materials such as plastic for example. It is possible to make plastic from the oil of plants such as oil seed rape. In fact, plants produce a range of different oils that could be put to many uses. It may even be possible to alter the plants genetically using gene technology to make them produce specific oils for particular purposes. However, some people would have concerns about the long-term environmental impact of such changes.

Oil seed rape produces seeds that have a high content of oil. This crop is usually harvested to make cooking oils and margarine, but increasingly the oil is made into bio-diesel for use in vehicles.

More durable goods

People should be encouraged to keep their belongings for longer, and not to replace consumer items such as phones, computers and televisions every few years. It has been found that longer guarantee periods encourage people to have products repaired rather than buy new ones. Therefore, a purchase tax could be charged on electrical goods sold with less than a five-year repair or replacement warranty. There could be laws requiring manufacturers to include a certain percentage of recycled content in their products in order to increase the demand for recyclable materials. Taxes could be introduced on materials that cannot be recycled.

Governments could lead the way by making suppliers meet higher environmental standards. Government purchasing has brought about a programme in Japan that requires buyers to think 'green' when making purchases. In the UK, government departments have targets for using recycled paper products and hybrid vehicles to reduce the use of fossil fuels. Hybrid vehicles have engines that are powered by a rechargeable battery and fuel, rather than just fuel. They are amongst the least polluting and most fuel-efficient vehicles on the road.

Closing the loop

It is important to remember that recycling has not actually taken place until we buy or use products made from recycled materials. For recycling schemes to be successful there must be a demand for recycled waste. This demand is created when people buy recycled goods. As well as helping the environment, buying recycled goods encourages investment in new industries and this creates new jobs. The process of buying recycled goods is called 'closing the loop'.

Case Study: Torop eco-village

The distinctive shape of the dome houses in Torop reduces both the materials required to build the house and the heat loss by 30 per cent. The large south facing windows let in light, and a wind turbine produces electricity for the homes.

The eco-village of Torop lies to the north of Copenhagen, Denmark. It was set up in 1990 and is home to about 150 people who live in houses that are visually striking and varied, and made from either renewable or recycled materials such as timber, straw bales and mud. All the houses are well insulated and make good use of solar energy. The aim was to create a community that included homes, shops, schools and businesses, a wind turbine and organic food production so that the community could be self-sufficient. The village has its own biological waste water cleaning system and gets its electricity from a 450-kilowatt wind turbine.

Denmark now has a number of similar projects, known as urban ecology projects.

What you can do to help

Taking action for the sustainable use of resources and reducing waste is becoming increasingly urgent in the 21st century. It is too easy to throw away materials that could be recycled. It is important that everybody thinks about recycling in order to reduce the amount of recyclable materials such as garden waste, glass and metal that end up in the rubbish bin.

We can all help to reduce waste by making simple changes in our lives. Having a compost heap in the garden where you can place kitchen and garden waste is one change you can make. Recycling as much rubbish as possible is another.

Organic matter such as kitchen waste and weeds from the garden can be tipped on to a compost heap where natural decomposers, such as fungi and bacteria, will break it down.

Thinking about your shopping

There are lots of things you can do to reduce waste when you go shopping. Firstly, take a bag with you rather than picking up new plastic bags at every shop you go into. Look carefully at the containers in which products are placed. Choose products in containers that can be recycled. Buy one large container rather than multiple small containers of the same thing. Some products are wrapped up in layers of unnecessary packaging, for example a box of chocolates or an Easter egg. This packaging helps to sell the product, but it is just thrown away. This is a complete waste of resources, so try to avoid products with excess packaging. Fruit and vegetables often come in layers of packaging too and so it is much better to buy from places where the produce is sold loose.

There are many one-use products on sale such as single-use cameras, disposable cutlery, paper plates and so on. Once these products have been used they are thrown away and new ones purchased. Avoid these products and pay a little more for something that you can use many times over instead.

When making decisions between two similar items, look to see if there is information about the recycled content. Try, wherever possible, to buy items made from recycled materials. Another choice would be to avoid those items that are difficult to recycle.

It may seem as if you are saving money by buying a cheaper product, but think about how long the product will last. It may be possible that a slightly more expensive one will last for longer.

Lastly, if you do not think a manufacturer is doing enough to cut waste find out where they are based and write to them and ask about their plans to cut waste.

Computers cannot easily be recycled because they contain harmful chemicals. When you're buying a new computer think about whether you really need a new one, and also about what happens to your old one.

45

Glossary

acid rain rain made acidic by polluting gases in the atmosphere, such as sulphur dioxide. Acid rain harms trees and water supplies, and damages buildings.

alloy chemical mix of two elements, one of which is a metal

biogas name given to the mix of gases produced by rotting organic matter. Biogas can be used as a fuel.

consumable items items that are meant to be used up and replaced

consumer goods goods purchased for personal use, for example televisions, computers, refrigerators

coolant liquid or gas used to cool a system by transferring heat away from one part to another

cullet crushed or broken glass for recycling

durability being hard-wearing. A durable product will last a long time.

emission substance, such as gas, given off or discharged. Carbon dioxide, for example, is an emission produced by the burning of fossil fuels such as coal.

fossil fuel substance such as coal, oil and natural gas, that is formed from the decayed remains of plants and animals. Fossil fuels release carbon dioxide when they are burned.

functionality how well something works

global warming gradual rise in temperature over all the Earth's surface caused by an increase in the concentration of greenhouse gases, such as carbon dioxide, methane and CFCs, in the atmosphere

impurity something that reduces the value of a substance

incinerator place where waste can be burned

ingot block of metal

landfill large hole in the ground used to dump waste

malleable capable of being shaped or burned

molten made into a liquid by heating

ore mineral from which a metal can be extracted

organic derived from living organisms

ozone chemical found high in the atmosphere that filters out harmful ultraviolet rays from sunlight

pesticide chemical used to kill pests, such as insects, on crops

pollutant substance that causes pollution

quarry place where rock is obtained from the ground by digging, cutting or blasting

raw material basic material from which a product is made. Oil is one of the raw materials of plastic.

recycle processing old, used items in order that the material can be used to make new products

refurbish repair something to bring it back into good working order

resource assets or materials that are valuable. The world's natural resources include water and fossil fuels such as coal, gas and oil.

retardant chemical that slows something down, for example chemicals that slow down the spread of a fire

sanitation provision of clean drinking water and adequate disposal of sewage (human waste)

silt fine sand, clay or other materials that is carried by water and often deposited in streams and rivers

textile type of material made from fibres

toxic poisonous

vapour type of gas

versatile able to adapt or be adapted to many different uses

Further information

Websites

Friends of the Earth

www.foe.org.uk

Environmental campaigning organisation that has a detailed website covering many environmental topics including issues associated with waste and recycling.

United States Environmental Protection Agency

http://www.epa.gov/osw

Lots of information on all types of waste, laws, what you can do and links to other sites.

Waste Online

www.wasteonline.org.uk

A comprehensive website looking at all forms of recycling, with facts and figures, information sheets and suggestions on how everybody can recycle more.

Plastics Recycling

http://www.plasticsrecycling.info

Website that gives lots of information about plastics, how they are made and used, and how they can be recycled.

British Glass

http://www.recyclingglass.co.uk

Website looking at glass and how it is recycled.

Can Smart

http://www.cansmart.org

Website of the steel can recycling campaign in Australia with news articles on recycling from around the world.

Waste Watch

http://www.wastewatch.org.uk

Waste Watch is a UK organisation that promotes and encourages waste reduction, reuse and recycling. Find lots of ideas and information about the things that you can do, and keep up with all of the latest news on waste.

World Wise Waste Guide

http://www.worldwise.com/wiseguide.html

This website has an online resource guide to help you understand more about sustainable living, with information on recycling and buying environmentally friendly products.

Books

21st Century Debates: Waste, Recycling and Reuse, Rob Bowden (Hodder Wayland, 2003)

Green Files: Waste and Recycling, Steve Parker (Heinemann Library, 2004)

Improving Our Environment: Waste and Recycling, Carol Inskipp (Hodder Wayland, 2005)

Material World: Separating Materials, Robert Sneddon (Heinemann Library, 2002)

Pachamama: Our Earth – Our Future (Evans Brothers, 2002)

Save cash and save the planet (Friends of the Earth, 2005)

Science Files: Textiles, Steve Parker (Heinemann Library, 2002)

Sustainable Human Development: A Young Person's Introduction, Peace Child International (Evans Brothers, 2003)

Polar Bear
Arctic Circle – Canada, Greenland, Norway, Russia, United States

Orchid Mantis
Southeast Asia

African Leopard
Sub-Saharan Africa

Mimic Octopus
Indo-Pacific Oceans – New Caledonia, Philippines, Thailand, Indonesia, Malaysia, Australia

Ornate Wobbegong
Pacific Ocean – Eastern Australia

Panther Chameleon
Madagascar

Leaf and Stick Insects
Australia

A NOTE FROM THE AUTHOR-ILLUSTRATOR

The animals hiding in these pages all have unique and impressive techniques for staying out of sight. Some change their colours and patterns to blend in with their surroundings, others disguise themselves as sticks or flowers and one even wears a cloak of algae!

While they might all have different approaches to camouflage, each is dependent on a unique environment to make its camouflage work. From the savannas of Africa to the jungles of South America to the waters of the Pacific Ocean, these places are necessary for their survival.

At a time when their habitats are under threat because of climate change and other human activities, it's up to us to make sure we do all that we can to protect these incredible masters of disguise – even when we can't always see them!

First published in Great Britain 2021 by Walker Books Ltd

87 Vauxhall Walk, London SE11 5HJ

2 4 6 8 10 9 7 5 3 1

© 2021 Marc Martin

The right of Marc Martin to be identified as author and illustrator of this work has been asserted by him in accordance with the Copyright, Designs and Patents Act 1988

This book has been typeset in Gill Sans Medium

Printed in China

British Library Cataloguing in Publication Data:

a catalogue record for this book is available from the British Library

ISBN 978-1-4063-9916-5

www.walkerstudio.com

MASTERS

· OF ·

DISGUISE

Can You Spot the Camouflaged Creatures?

Marc Martin

WALKER ❚ STUDIO
AN IMPRINT OF WALKER BOOKS

Panther Chameleon

Chameleons are known for their remarkable ability to change colour to blend into their environment. These reptiles are often found in the treetops of tropical or mountain rainforests and grassland. Madagascar is home to almost half of the world's chameleon species, including the panther chameleon, one of fifty-nine chameleon species found nowhere else on the planet.

360-Degree View

Chameleons can rotate each eye nearly 180 degrees and focus each one independently, which means they can look at two things at once!

A Kaleidoscope of Colours

Like many chameleons, a panther chameleon can change colour with the help of special cells in their skin called chromatophores. These cells help the chameleon blend in with its environment and evade predators. It can also take on brighter colours to intimidate rivals or communicate with potential mates.

Sticky Situation

Not only is a chameleon's tongue about twice its body length, but a chameleon can shoot its tongue out of its mouth and hit its prey in about 0.007 seconds!

A Firm Grasp

Chameleons' five toes have evolved into groups. The forefoot has two outside toes joined together to form one group, and three inside toes form another; the hind foot has the opposite arrangement. This allows them to grasp branches and keep a grip while climbing.

Kaleidoscopic Camouflage

Have you heard of the helmet vanga, Schlegel's asity, red fody, comet moth or tomato frog? They are just some of the unique creatures hiding in this forest, along with ten cleverly concealed chameleons!

Great Horned Owl

The great horned owl is the most common owl in the Americas, ranging from Alaska to Argentina. They live in many habitats, including forests, scrublands, marshes, deserts and even urban areas.

Silent but Deadly

The owls' feathers are loosely packed and have soft saw-toothed edges that allow the birds to fly almost silently, making them stealthy hunters that can sneak up on their prey.

Grip

When clenched, the owls' strong talons require a force of 13 kilograms (28 pounds) to open. They use their grip to kill and carry prey several times heavier than themselves, such as falcons, ospreys and raccoons.

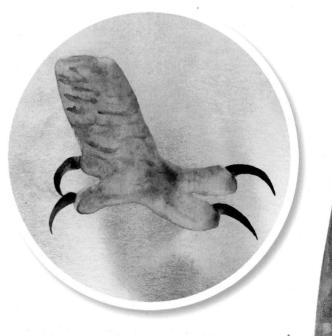

Eyes Everywhere

The great horned owls' large eyes have pupils that can open widely in the dark for excellent night vision. While their eyes don't move in their sockets, they can swivel their heads more than 180 degrees to look in any direction.

Plumicorns

The great horned owl gets its name from the tufts of feathers on its head called plumicorns. While these tufts look like ears, its ears are actually tiny openings lower down on the skull, hidden beneath feathers.

Stealth Hearing

A concave arrangement of facial feathers helps direct sound to their ears. Their hearing is so good they can hear a mouse stepping on a twig 23 metres (75 feet) away!

Patterned Feathers

The great horned owls' mottled and striped feathers allow them to blend into the surrounding tree bark.

Whoooo's There?

Squirrels, black bears, elk, ruby-crowned kinglets and acorn woodpeckers all share this redwood forest with the great horned owl. Can you see all eleven owls hiding in tree hollows and blending into their surroundings?

Polar Bear

Polar bears live on ice-covered waters around the Arctic Circle, inhabiting parts of Canada, Greenland, Norway, Russia and the United States. The sea ice provides them with access to food (primarily seals) and a place to rest and breed, but melting ice – a result of climate change – means their habitat is shrinking fast.

Big Foot

With paws measuring up to 30 centimetres (12 inches) across, polar bears' giant feet act like snowshoes and distribute their weight on thin ice and deep snow. Their footpads have small bumps called papillae, which stop them from sliding on the slippery ice, and their long curved claws provide extra grip and grabbing power.

Black *and* White

The hairs of a polar bear are colourless and hollow and only appear white because of the way light refracts through the fur – the skin underneath is actually black! This white-looking fur helps a polar bear blend in with its snow and ice environment, allowing it to sneak up on unsuspecting prey.

Marine Mammals

Polar bears are the only bears to be considered marine mammals because they spend so much of their lives on sea ice rather than land. They can run up to 40 kilometres (25 miles) per hour on land in short bursts, swim around 10 kilometres (6 miles) and hold their breath for more than two minutes. In fact, their Latin name, *Ursus maritimus*, translates to "sea bear"!

A Spotless Coat

After eating, polar bears will often roll in snow or go for a swim to clean their coat. Keeping their fur clean helps protect the insulating properties of their coat and maintain that spotless white they need for camouflage.

Sniffing Out a Meal

Polar bears can smell a seal from more than 1 kilometre (half a mile) away or even when their prey is hiding under 1 metre (3 feet) of snow!

Colours of the Arctic

Seals, Arctic terns, kittiwakes and common eiders all coexist on the Arctic plains, with the threat of polar bears sniffing them out! There are ten polar bears in this landscape – can you see them all?

Leaf and Stick Insects

Leaf and stick insects, also known as phasmids, use their leaf-and twig-shaped bodies to camouflage themselves into surrounding trees. There are around three thousand phasmid species, 150 of which are found in Australia, including the children's stick insect, the spiny leaf insect and the gargantuan stick insect.

Motion Masquerade

Leaf insects typically sway back and forth when hanging on branches to mimic foliage rustling in the wind and avoid detection by predators.

Leafy Camouflage

The children's stick insect lives on eucalyptus trees and feeds on their leaves. The long yellow strip that runs down the centre of its body makes it look almost exactly like a eucalyptus leaf and helps it hide from predators.

Parthenogenesis

Many phasmids are able to reproduce via parthenogenesis. In this process, a female phasmid produces offspring without a male mate, laying eggs that hatch only females.

Gargantuan Giant

Measuring around 50 centimetres (20 inches) long, the gargantuan stick insect is one of the longest insects in the world. These elusive climbers are extremely rare, and their stick-like bodies make them all the more difficult to find amid the forest canopy.

Peanut Butter Defense

The spiny leaf insect is typically found hanging from trees, its body resembling a dried leaf amid the foliage. When threatened, adults produce an odour that smells like peanut butter or toffee to humans, but smells unpleasant to predators.

Stick or Insect?

Kookaburras, koalas, rainbow lorikeets and yellow-crested black cockatoos all like a good perch. There are ten children's stick insects, five gargantuan stick insects and two spiny leaf insects among these eucalyptus trees. Can you find them all?

Owl Butterfly

Owl butterflies are primarily found in the rainforests of Central and South America and Mexico. The eye-shaped circles on their wings resemble the eyes of an owl. These eyespots may scare predators away or confuse the predator to aim for the "eye" on the lower part of the wing and not the body, thus giving the butterfly a greater chance of escape.

Hanging Around

Owl butterflies are crepuscular, which means they are most active at sunrise and sunset. During the day they rest on leaves with their wings held tightly together.

A Flashy Side

The markings on one side of owl butterflies' wings resemble tree bark, while the other side has flashes of purplish blue and yellow, which may startle a predator.

Spread Your Wings

Owl butterflies are one of the largest butterflies in Central America, with a wingspan of up to 20 centimetres (8 inches). In fact, their wings are so big that they tend to fly only a few yards at a time before needing a rest!

Life Cycle

1. Egg

Butterfly eggs are very small and are laid on plants by the female. These plants then become food for the hatching caterpillars (also known as larvae).

2. Larva (Caterpillar)

Several days after the eggs are laid, caterpillars emerge and gorge themselves on leaves. As a caterpillar grows, it sheds its skin four or five times.

3. Pupa

When a caterpillar is fully grown, it stops eating, attaches itself to a branch and forms a pupa (also known as a chrysalis). This cocoon resembles the head of a viper snake, another deterrent for predators! Within the chrysalis the caterpillar changes in a process called metamorphosis. It grows wings, legs and eyes and transforms into a butterfly.

4. Butterfly

When the butterfly first emerges from the chrysalis, its wings are soft and folded against its body. It pumps blood into the wings to get them working so it can fly and find a mate to start the life cycle again.

Who's Looking at You?

Not all eyes are what they seem! Hiding from the gaze of keel-billed toucans, squirrel monkeys, slender sheartails and yellow-winged tanagers are seventeen owl butterflies! Don't forget to look for the patterns on both sides of their wings!

African Leopard

The African leopard is found in sub-Saharan Africa, from mountainous forests to grasslands and savannas. They are powerful big cats, closely related to lions, tigers and jaguars.

Spots

Leopards' spots help them blend into their surroundings – tall grasses and dappled sunlight when on the ground or leaves when climbing in trees. This spotted camouflage helps them get close to their prey before they pounce.

Black Roses

The spots on a leopard's coat are called rosettes because their shape is similar to that of a rose. There are also black leopards (sometimes referred to as black panthers) whose spots are hard to see because of their dark fur, although these types of leopards are more common in Asia.

Spring into Action

Leopards are fast felines and can run up to 58 kilometres (36 miles) per hour. When hunting, they spring into action and can leap 6 metres (20 feet) and 3 metres (10 feet) straight up.

Tree Fridge

Leopards are the strongest climbers of all the big cats and will often store carcasses up trees. They are capable of carrying animals heavier than themselves up trees to protect the carcasses from scavengers.

Lone Hunter

Leopards are solitary animals and spend most of their time alone. They are also nocturnal, hunting for prey at night, and spend most of their days resting, camouflaged in trees or hiding in caves.

Leisurely Lying Low

African leopards are most active between sunset and sunrise, when they hunt for prey – giant eland, kudu, springboks and even giraffes all have to be on the lookout! There are fifteen leopards waiting for the light to fade so they can pounce into action!

Three-Toed Sloth

The three-toed sloth is the world's slowest mammal. In fact, it's so slow that algae grows on its furry coat! The green algae makes the sloth's fur look a little green, which means it can blend in with the trees of the Central and South American rainforests where it lives.

A Leisurely Pace

Sloths move through the forest canopy at a mere 1.8–2.4 metres (6–8 feet) per minute, eating leaves, buds and fruits. They also have very low metabolic rates, taking them a long time to convert food into energy, and can spend ten to fifteen hours a day sleeping.

Symbiotic Relationship

The algae camouflages the sloth, but what's in it for the algae? The sloth's fur provides the algae with a healthy supply of water because sloth fur is very absorbent. They have a symbiotic relationship, meaning each creature depends on the other for something it needs.

Hanging Out

Sloths are arboreal animals, meaning they spend nearly all their time in trees, gripping branches with the help of their long, powerful claws. They descend to the ground only to find a mate, establish new territory or poo (which they do only once a week!).

Speedy Swimmers

Sloths' long arms make them surprisingly good swimmers! Swimming helps them travel faster and further when searching for a mate or looking for new territory.

Slow Food Movement

Sloths conserve movement and metabolize their food slowly – it can take up to a month for a sloth to digest one meal! This means they are rarely hungry and don't need to compete with other animals as often for food.

Slothful Swaying

Three-toed sloths spend most of their time suspended in the treetops among birds like the hyacinth macaw, red-and-green macaw, plum-throated cotinga and oropendola. Can you spot all twelve sloths in this rainforest?

Mimic Octopus

Mimic octopuses are predominantly found in shallow river mouths and estuaries of the Indo-Pacific, from New Caledonia, the Philippines, Thailand, Indonesia and Malaysia to as far south as the Great Barrier Reef in Australia.

Amazing Actor

It's estimated that the mimic octopus can imitate around fifteen animals, including sea snakes, stingrays, lionfish, jellyfish, poisonous flatfish, sole, eels, starfish and coral. It is the only known marine animal able to mimic such a wide variety of ocean life.

The primary purpose of this mimicry is protection from predators (as most of the animals it imitates are poisonous or bad-tasting). However, the mimic octopus can also imitate species such as crabs to get close to prey before pouncing.

Colour and Contortion

The mimic octopus can change its skin colour and texture using cells equipped with pigment sacs called chromatophores. This ability to blend in with its environment, combined with the ability to contort its body to take on the appearance of other animals, makes it a master impersonator.

Master Impersonator

1. Jellyfish: The octopus spreads its arms and lets them gently float in the water to resemble a jellyfish.

2. Sole: The octopus pulls its arms in and flattens its body to mimic a sole.

3. Lionfish: The octopus spreads out its arms to resemble the lionfish's venomous brown-and-white spines.

4. Sea Snake: The octopus pulls six of its arms into a burrow and leaves two out to resemble the venomous sea snake.

Choosing Its Roles

The mimic octopus chooses which animal to impersonate based on which predator is nearby. For example, if bullied by a territorial damselfish, it will mimic a sea snake, a well-known predator of the damselfish.

A Variety of Disguises

In the shallows and estuaries of the ocean you might find stingrays, manta rays, great barracuda, sailfin snapper and orangespine unicornfish ... but can you find the eight mimic octopuses?

Brown Vine Snake

The brown vine snake is usually found hanging in trees or low shrubs, where, as its name suggests, it is easily mistaken for a vine. It inhabits mostly arid environments, including dry forest edges, thickets, wooded grasslands, brushy hillsides and densely vegetated canyons. Its habitat ranges from southern Arizona in the United States through Mexico to northern South America and Trinidad and Tobago.

Sticking Around

Remaining motionless, vine snakes disguise themselves as vines or sticks and wait to pounce on unsuspecting prey. They will sometimes flick their bright-coloured tongue back and forth to use it as a lure; the motion attracts insects that mistake the tongue for a worm.

Everything is Just Vine

Very thin and vine-like in appearance, the brown vine snake can grow up to 2 metres (6 feet) long. Its various shades of grey, silver and copper help it blend in with its surroundings.

Rear-Fanged

The brown vine snake is rear-fanged, or opisthoglyphous, meaning its fangs are found at the back of the upper jaw rather than at the front, like other snake species. It uses venom to kill its prey, but is only mildly venomous and not considered dangerous to humans. Its main prey are lizards, but it will occasionally eat insects, frogs and birds.

Open Wide!

If in danger, the vine snake will sometimes hold its mouth wide open, exposing the dark lining within to make itself look larger and more threatening.

Defensive Farting

When threatened, the vine snake will sometimes release foul-smelling secretions from the vent on the bottom of its tail.

Stealthy Slithering

Brown vine snakes like to hang very still from trees and branches until unsuspecting prey comes along. In these shrubs you will find bronzed cowbirds, cardinals, eastern meadowlarks, sparrows, frogs, lizards and twelve snakes!

Gaboon Viper

Gaboon vipers are usually found in rainforests and woodlands of Central, East and West Africa. They are terrestrial snakes, meaning they stay on the ground and don't climb trees like some other snakes.

Hinged Fangs for Storage

A viper's fangs are attached to the jaw by a hinge, so they can be folded up against the roof of the mouth when not in use. This folding action allows the Gaboon viper to have the longest fangs of any venomous snake in the world! Its fangs can grow up to 5 centimetres (2 inches) in length and its large venom glands produce the largest quantity of venom of any venomous snake.

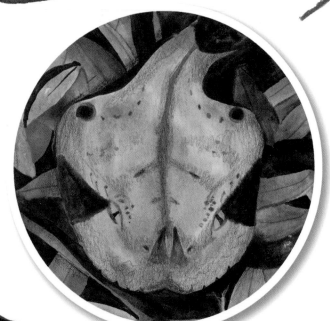

Leaf Head

The Gaboon viper's leaf-shaped head is marked with a dark central vein, much like a fallen leaf. Their bodies are patterned with rectangles and triangles of light yellow, purple and brown, which help them blend seamlessly with leaves and roots on the forest floor.

Big Snake

Gaboon vipers are the largest vipers in Africa, weighing up to 20 kilograms (45 pounds) and reaching lengths of more than 2 metres (6 feet). Some vipers even have heads of nearly 15 centimetres (6 inches)! Because of their large bodies, adults can eat prey as large as fully grown rabbits.

Hunting by Ambush

Primarily nocturnal, Gaboon vipers are slow-moving and generally unaggressive snakes. They hunt mostly by ambush, disappearing into the forest floor and waiting for suitable prey to pass within striking distance.

A Predator Underfoot

The Gaboon viper shares its rainforest habitat with many animals – African forest elephants, okapis and chimpanzees all have to watch where they step! Can you find all eleven vipers on this page?

Ornate Wobbegong

The ornate wobbegong is a species of shark that is mostly found in the Pacific Ocean near eastern Australia. Its patterned markings allow it to hide among plants and reefs, making it the perfect camouflaged predator! Wobbegongs are also referred to as carpet sharks because they are bottom-dwelling sharks that stay close to the ocean floor.

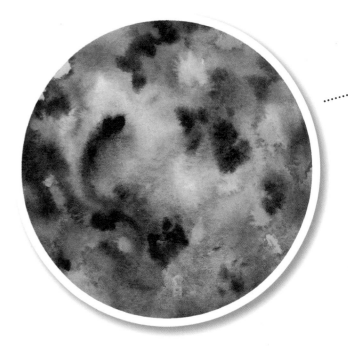

Shaggy Beard

Wobbegongs have whiskers and skin flaps, called barbels, around their nose and mouth that resemble plant-like growths. This bearded fringe acts as both camouflage and bait for the small fish it feeds on.

Watch Your Step!

Ornate wobbegongs usually don't bite humans. However, because they're so well camouflaged, swimmers and divers often fail to see them and sometimes accidentally touch or step on them, making them a little angry!

The Art of Ambush

Wobbegongs patiently wait for prey to come close ... and then pounce with a quick snap! They swallow small prey whole, or if the prey is too large, they hold it within their jaws (sometimes for days) until it dies. Then they can eat without a fight!

Night Owl

The wobbegong is nocturnal, meaning it's most active at night. During the day it rests out in the open or under rocks and ledges. Although it has poor eyesight, it can use its barbels to sense its environment.

Walk on Water

Wobbegongs can move across the ocean floor using their bottom fins, giving them the appearance of walking. Some have been seen climbing out of the water from one tide pool to another. As long as their gills are wet, they can survive this quick adventure!

Immersive Experience

Ornate wobbegongs use their markings to blend in with the reefs and plants around them. Triggerfish, blue tangs, humphead wrasse, giant trevallies and groupers all swim around as twelve wobbegongs stealthily stay out of sight!

Orchid Mantis

Found in the rainforests of Southeast Asia, the orchid mantis is one of several species known as flower mantises because of their striking resemblance to flowers. They wait patiently on branches to catch small insects such as crickets, flies, butterflies and bees.

Aggressive Mimicry

Using a special type of camouflage called aggressive mimicry, the orchid mantis doesn't try to hide to lure its prey, but instead stands out and mimics the look of a flower. Insects are attracted to what they think is a meal, only to be eaten for lunch!

Not an Orchid

Orchid mantises aren't actually trying to imitate a particular orchid. By having coloured markings that suggest a "generic" flower, or a close approximation of several different flowers rather than an identical match of a specific species, they are able to lure more types of prey.

A Firm Hold

Mantises have spiky saw-toothed forelegs that help them hold on tight to caught prey.

Deadly Hunter

The mantis climbs up twigs and branches and waits patiently for prey by imitating a flower. It clings to a perch with its two back legs, sways from side to side to look more enticing and quickly snatches prey with its front legs once in reach.

Changing Colours

By detecting changing light and humidity, the mantis can adapt its colour to resemble surrounding flowers within a few days, changing between white, pink, yellow and purple.

Changing Hues

Birds like the whiskered treeswift, jambu fruit dove, Raffles's malkoha and scarlet-rumped trogon love an orchid mantis snack! Can you find all thirteen mantises before they do?

Great Horned Owl
North and South America

Brown Vine Snake
*Southern Arizona (United States),
Mexico, northern South America,
and Trinidad and Tobago*

Owl Butterfly
*Mexico, Central and
South America*

Three-Toed Sloth
Central and South America

Gaboon Viper
Central, East and West Africa